MACBETH

Shakespeare: The Animated Tales is a multinational venture conceived by S4C, Channel 4 Wales. Produced in Russia, Wales, and England, the series has been financed by S4C, the BBC, and HIT Communications (UK), Christmas Films and Soyuzmultfilm (Russia), Home Box Office (USA), and Fujisankei (Japan).

Academic Panel
Professor Stanley Wells
Dr. Rex Gibson

Academic Co-ordinator
Roy Kendall

Educational Adviser
Michael Marland

Publishing Editor and Co-ordinator
Jane Fior

Book Design
Fiona Macmillan

Animation Director for *Macbeth*
Nikolai Serebriakov of Soyuzmultfilm Studios, Moscow

Series Producer and Director
Dave Edwards of The Dave Edwards Studio Ltd, Cardiff, Wales

Executive Producers
Christopher Grace
Elizabeth Babakhina

Library of Congress Cataloging-in-Publication Data
Garfield, Leon.
    Macbeth / abridged by Leon Garfield ; illustrated by Nikolai
Serebriakov.
        p.   cm. — (Shakespeare, the animated tales)
    Summary: An illustrated, abridged version of Shakespeare's historical
tragedy with background information and explanatory stage directions.
    ISBN 0–679–83875–9 (pbk.) — ISBN 0–679–93875–3 (lib. bdg.)
    1. Macbeth, King of Scotland, 11th cent.—Juvenile drama.
2. Children's plays, English. [1. Macbeth, King of Scotland, 11th cent.—
Drama. 2. Plays.]
    I. Serebriakov, Nikolia, ill. II. Shakespeare, William, 1564–1616. Macbeth.
III. Title. IV. Series: Garfield, Leon. Shakespeare, the animated tales.
PR2823.A25   1993
822.3′3—dc20   92–14521

Shakespeare

MACBETH

ABRIDGED BY LEON GARFIELD

ILLUSTRATED BY NIKOLAI SEREBRIAKOV

ALFRED A. KNOPF NEW YORK

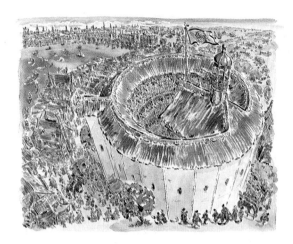

THE THEATRE IN SHAKESPEARE'S DAY

IN 1989 AN ARCHAEOLOGICAL discovery was made on the south bank of the Thames that sent shivers of delight through the theatre world. A fragment of Shakespeare's own theatre, the Globe, where many of his plays were first performed, had been found.

This discovery has fuelled further interest in how Shakespeare himself conceived and staged his plays. We know a good deal already, and archaeology as well as documentary research will no doubt reveal more, but although we can only speculate on some of the details, we have a good idea of what the Elizabethan theatre-goer saw, heard and smelt when he went to see a play by William Shakespeare at the Globe.

It was an entirely different experience from anything we know today. Modern theatres have roofs to keep out the weather. If it rained on the Globe, forty per cent of the play-goers got wet. Audiences today sit on cushioned seats, and usually (especially if the play is by Shakespeare) watch and listen in respectful silence. In the Globe, the floor of the theatre was packed with a riotous crowd of garlic-reeking apprentices, house servants and artisans, who had each paid a penny to stand for the entire duration of the play, to buy nuts and apples from the food-sellers, to refresh themselves with bottled ale, relieve themselves, perhaps, into buckets by the back wall, to talk, cheer, catcall, clap and hiss if the play did not please them.

In the galleries, that rose in curved tiers around the inside of the building, sat those who could afford to pay two pennies for a seat, and the benefits of a roof over their heads. Here, the middle ranking citizens, the merchants, the sea captains, the clerks from the Inns of Court, would sit crammed into their small eighteen inch space and look down upon the 'groundlings' below. In the 'Lords room', the rich and the great, noblemen and women, courtiers and foreign ambassadors had to pay sixpence each for the relative comfort and luxury of their exclusive position directly above the stage, where they smoked tobacco, and overlooked the rest.

We are used to a stage behind an arch, with wings on either side, from which the actors come on and into which they disappear. In the Globe, the stage was a platform thrusting out into the middle of the floor, and the audience, standing in the central yard, surrounded it on three sides. There were no wings. Three doors at the back of the stage were used for all exits and entrances. These were sometimes covered by a curtain, which could be used as a prop.

Today we sit in a darkened theatre or cinema, and look at a brilliantly lit stage or screen, or we sit at home in a small, private world of our own, watching a luminous television screen. The close-packed, rowdy crowd at the Globe, where the play started at two o'clock in the afternoon, had no artificial light to enhance their illusion. It was the words that moved them. They came to listen, rather than to see.

No dimming lights announced the start of the play. A blast from a trumpet and three sharp knocks warned the audience that the action was about to begin. In the broad daylight, the actor could see the audience as clearly as the audience could see him. He spoke directly to the crowd, and held them with his eyes, following their reactions. He could play up to the raucous laughter that greeted the comical, bawdy scenes, and gauge the emotional response to the higher flights of poetry. Sometimes he even improvised speeches of his own. He was surrounded by, enfolded by his audience.

The stage itself would seem uncompromisingly bare to our eyes. There was no scenery. No painted backdrops suggested a forest, or a castle, or the sumptuous interior of a palace. Shakespeare painted the scenery with his words, and the imagination of the audience did the rest.

Props were brought onto the stage only when they were essential for the action. A bed would be carried on when a character needed to lie on it. A throne would be let down from above when a king needed to sit on it. Torches and lanterns would suggest that it was dark, but the main burden of persuading an audience, at three o'clock in the afternoon, that it was in fact the middle of the night, fell upon the language.

Thus in *Macbeth*, the king evokes the darkness: 'Come, seeling night, scarf up the tender eye of pitiful day.' Shakespeare's actors were responsible for their own costumes. They would use what was to hand in the 'tiring house' (dressing room), or supplement it out of their own pockets. Classical, medieval and Tudor clothes could easily appear side by side in the same play.

No women actors appeared on a public stage until many years after

Shakespeare's death, for at that time it would have been considered shameless. The parts of young girls were played by boys. The parts of older women were played by older men.

In 1613 the Globe theatre was set on fire by a spark from a cannon during a performance of Henry VIII, and it burnt to the ground. The actors, including Shakespeare himself, dug into their own pockets and paid for it to be rebuilt. The new theatre lasted until 1642, when it closed again. Now, in the 1990s, the Globe is set to rise again as a committed band of actors, scholars and enthusiasts are raising the money to rebuild Shakespeare's theatre in its original form a few yards from its previous site.

From the time when the first Globe theatre was built until today, Shakespeare's plays have been performed in a vast variety of languages, styles, costumes and techniques, on stage, on film, on television and in animated film. Shakespeare himself, working within the round wooden walls of his theatre, would have been astonished by it all.

Patrick Spottiswoode
Director Globe Education,
Shakespeare Globe Trust

WILLIAM SHAKESPEARE

NEXT TO GOD, A wise man once said, Shakespeare created most. In the thirty-seven plays that are his chief legacy to the world—and surely no-one ever left a richer!—human nature is displayed in all its astonishing variety.

He has enriched the stage with matchless comedies, tragedies, histories, and, towards the end of his life, with plays that defy all description, strange plays that haunt the imagination like visions.

His range is enormous: kings and queens, priests, princes and merchants, soldiers, clowns and drunkards, murderers, pimps, whores, fairies, monsters and pale, avenging ghosts 'strut and fret their hour upon the stage'. Murders and suicides abound; swords flash, blood flows, poison drips, and lovers sigh; yet there is always time for old men to talk of growing apples and for gardeners to discuss the weather.

In the four hundred years since they were written, they have become known and loved in every land; they are no longer the property of one country and one people, they are the priceless possession of the world.

His life, from what we know of it, was not astonishing. The stories that have attached themselves to him are remarkable only for their ordinariness: poaching deer, sleeping off a drinking bout under a wayside tree. There are no duels, no loud, passionate loves, no excesses of any kind. He was not one of your unruly geniuses whose habits are more interesting than their works. From all accounts, he was of a gentle, honourable disposition, a good businessman, and a careful father.

He was born on April 23rd 1564, to John and Mary Shakespeare of Henley Street, Stratford-upon-Avon. He was their third child and first son. When he was four or five he began his education at the local petty school. He left the local grammar school when he was about fourteen, in all probability to help in his father's glove-making shop. When he was eighteen, he married Anne Hathaway, who lived in a nearby village. By the time he was twenty-one, he was the father of three children, two daughters and a son.

Then, it seems, a restless mood came upon him. Maybe he travelled, maybe he was, as some say, a schoolmaster in the country; but at some time during the next seven years, he went to London and found employment in the theatre. When he was twenty-eight, he was already well enough known as an actor and playwright to excite the spiteful envy of a rival, who referred to him as 'an upstart crow'.

He mostly lived and worked in London until his mid-forties, when he returned to his family and home in Stratford, where he remained in prosperous circumstances until his death on April 23rd 1616, his fifty-second birthday.

He left behind him a widow, two daughters (his son died in childhood), and the richest imaginary world ever created by the human mind.

MACBETH

This is one of the darkest of Shakespeare's plays, and perhaps the most terrifying play ever written. Set in ancient Scotland, it is a tale of witchcraft, murder and madness. It is the tale of a great soldier who is tempted by wicked prophecies into seizing the crown of Scotland by murdering the king.

Shakespeare wrote the play when he was about forty-two. He found the story in Ralph Holinshed's *Chronicles of England, Scotland and Ireland*, and altered it to suit his dramatic purposes. It is one of the shortest of the plays, and by far the most concentrated.

Macbeth himself dominates it; all others, even his 'fiend-like queen', pale beside his huge presence; and we watch, in horrified fascination, as he, with eyes wide open, and knowing all the consequences, chooses evil instead of good; for his creed is the most dangerous of all: 'for mine own good all causes shall give way.'

It is a play about evil; and evil rises from it like a poisoned fog, choking out all light. Black is its prevailing colour, relieved only by the red glare of blood. 'Who would have thought the old man to have had so much blood in him?' wonders Lady Macbeth, walking in her hideous sleep, as she and her murderous husband go their divided ways to the 'everlasting bonfire'.

LEON GARFIELD

THE CHARACTERS IN THE PLAY

in order of appearance

FIRST WITCH	
SECOND WITCH	
THIRD WITCH	
DUNCAN	*King of Scotland*
MACBETH	*Thane of Glamis, later of Cawdor, later King of Scotland*
BANQUO	
ROSSE	*Thanes of Scotland*
ANGUS	
LADY MACBETH	
SERVANT	*to Lady Macbeth*
MACDUFF	*Thanes of Scotland*
LENNOX	
DONALBAIN	*Sons to Duncan*
MALCOLM	
FLEANCE	*Banquo's son*
LORDS	
MURDERER	
FIRST APPARITION	
SECOND APPARITION	
THIRD APPARITION	
DOCTOR	
WOMAN	*attendant on Lady Macbeth*
FIRST NOBLE	
SECOND NOBLE	
COURTIER	
SOLDIER	

The curtain rises on a wild heath under a dark, ragged sky. Thunder and lightning. Three hideous old women, huddled together, screaming with malignant laughter.

1ST WITCH   When shall we three meet again? In thunder, lightning, or in rain?

2ND WITCH   When the hurly-burly's done, when the battle's lost and won!

1ST WITCH   Where the place?

2ND WITCH   Upon the heath!

3RD WITCH   There to meet with Macbeth!

They stare at one another, and nod.

ALL   Fair is foul and foul is fair: hover through the fog and filthy air!

Thunder and lighting. The witches vanish.

The battle is for Scotland itself. Norway has invaded. In the midst of the mad confusion of battle, the gigantic figures of Macbeth and Banquo, his companion-in-arms, lay about them with ceaseless swords. They are the great generals of Duncan, lawful king of Scotland. Presently the battle subsides. The survivors cheer and raise their swords and spears to Macbeth, the victor. He waves his sword in acknowledgement; and Banquo, taking up a drum from a fallen boy, rattles out a roll of triumph.

In the royal camp, good king Duncan learns with joy of Macbeth's victory; but at the same time, hears of the treachery of the Thane of Cawdor, who has been captured. Sadly, he shakes his head.

DUNCAN There's no art to find the mind's construction in the face. He was a gentleman on whom I built an absolute trust. Go pronounce his present death, and with his former title greet Macbeth. What he hath lost, noble Macbeth hath won.

The heath. Madman's weather! Macbeth and Banquo are on their way to the royal camp.

MACBETH So fair and foul a day I have not seen.

Suddenly they halt. Their way is barred by three hideous old women!

BANQUO	What are these, withered and so wild in their attire?

They do not answer. Banquo thumps on his drum.

BANQUO	Live you? Or are you aught that man may question?

One by one, the witches raise their skinny fingers to their lips.
They gaze at Macbeth.

MACBETH	Speak if you can! What are you?
1ST WITCH	All hail, Macbeth, hail to thee, Thane of Glamis!

Banquo thumps in agreement.

2ND WITCH	All hail, Macbeth, hail to thee, Thane of Cawdor!

Banquo, drumsticks raised, hesitates.

3RD WITCH	All hail, Macbeth, that shalt be king hereafter!

The drumsticks fall. Macbeth bends to pick them up.

BANQUO	If you can look into the seeds of time and say which grain will grow, and which will not, speak then to me.
1ST WITCH	Lesser than Macbeth and greater.
2ND WITCH	Not so happy, yet much happier.
3RD WITCH	Thou shalt get kings though thou be none!

With each pronouncement, Macbeth taps humorously on Banquo's drum; but with the last, his blow is violent and splits the drumskin. The rent is in the form of a dagger! Macbeth and Banquo stare at it. As they do so, the witches vanish.

BANQUO   The earth hath bubbles, as the water has, and these are of them—

MACBETH   Your children shall be kings.

BANQUO   You shall be king—

MACBETH   —And Thane of Cawdor too; went it not so?

As they stare into the terrible air, two ghostly figures appear. As they draw near, they are seen to be two messengers from the king: Rosse and Angus. They salute Macbeth.

ROSSE   The king hath happily received, Macbeth, the news of thy success. Everyone did bear thy praises, in his kingdom's great defence, and poured them down before him. He bade me, from him, call thee Thane of Cawdor!

BANQUO   (*aside*) What! Can the Devil speak true?

MACBETH   The Thane of Cawdor lives; why do you dress me in borrowed robes?

ANGUS   Who was the Thane lives yet; but under heavy judgement bears that life which he deserves to lose.

Macbeth, in high excitement, turns aside.

MACBETH   Glamis, and Thane of Cawdor! Two truths are told, as happy prologues to the swelling act of the imperial theme! Stars, hide your fires! Let not light see my black and deep desires!

At Inverness, in the castle of Macbeth, his wife reads a letter from her husband. It tells of the meeting with the Weird Sisters and their marvellous prophecies, one of which has already come true. She puts aside the letter and paces the room.

LADY MACBETH   Glamis thou art, and Cawdor, and shalt be what thou art promised.—Yet do I fear thy nature; it is too full of the milk of human kindness, to catch the nearest way. Thou wouldst be great, art not without ambition, but without the illness should attend it. Hie thee hither that I may pour my spirits in thine ear—

Comes a knocking on the door. A servant enters.

LADY MACBETH   What's your tidings?

SERVANT   The King comes here tonight—

LADY MACBETH   Thou'rt mad to say it!

SERVANT   So please you, it is true.

She dismisses the servant. She is alone. The harsh cry of a raven causes her to start. Her eyes blaze with a terrible desire.

LADY MACBETH   The raven himself is hoarse that croaks the fatal entrance of Duncan under my battlements! Come, you spirits that tend on mortal thoughts, unsex me here, and fill me, from the crown to the toe, top-full of direst cruelty! Come to my woman's breasts, and take my milk for gall, you murdering ministers—

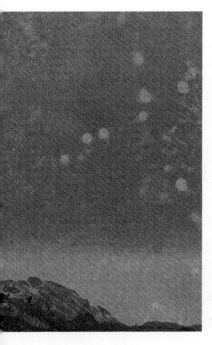

The door bursts open. Macbeth, still blood-stained from battle, stands before her.

LADY MACBETH   Great Glamis, worthy Cawdor, greater than both by the all-hail hereafter!

MACBETH   My dearest love, Duncan comes here tonight.

LACY MACBETH   And when goes hence?

MACBETH   Tomorrow, as he purposes.

LADY MACBETH   O never shall sun that morrow see! Your face, my thane, is as a book where men may read strange matters. To beguile the time look like the time, bear welcome in your eye, your hand, your tongue; look like the innocent flower, but be the serpent under't. He that's coming must be provided for; and you shall put this night's great business into my dispatch, which shall to all our nights and days to come give solely sovereign sway and masterdom.

MACBETH   (*uncertainly*) We will speak further—

LADY MACBETH Only look up clear; leave all the rest to me.

The courtyard of the castle. King Duncan, accompanied by his sons, Malcolm and Donalbain, and a train of nobles and servants, has arrived. Lady Macbeth greets him with loyal smiles and humble curtsies.

DUNCAN   Conduct me to mine host; we love him highly.

Evening. A banquet is in progress to honour the royal guest. The door of the dining-chamber opens briefly and a dark figure emerges. It is Macbeth. He is deeply disturbed.

MACBETH
If it were done, when 'tis done, then 'twere well it were done quickly: if the assassination could trammel up the consequence . . .? He's here in double trust; first as I am his kinsman and his subject, strong both against the deed; then as his host who should against his murderer shut the door, not bear the knife myself. Besides, this Duncan hath borne his faculties so meek, hath been so clear in his great office, that his virtues will plead like angels, trumpet-tongued, against the deep damnation of his taking-off—

The door opens and closes again. Lady Macbeth has followed him, leaving King Duncan at the banquet table.

LADY MACBETH
Why have you left the chamber?

MACBETH
We will proceed no further in this business.

LADY MACBETH
Art thou afeard to be the same in thine own act and valour as thou art in desire?

MACBETH
Prithee, peace! I dare do all that may become a man, who dares do more is none.

LADY MACBETH
What beast was't then that made you break this enterprise to me?

MACBETH   If we should fail?

LADY MACBETH   We fail? But screw your courage to the sticking-place and we'll not fail!

Night. The great hall of the castle. All is quiet. A flickering light appears. Macbeth, with a servant, bearing a torch. They halt.

MACBETH   Go bid thy mistress, when my drink is ready, she strike upon the bell.

The servant departs, leaving the torch to glimmer on the spears and shields that hang upon the wall. Its light, reflected on the polished surfaces, seems to form the shapes of daggers . . .

MACBETH: Is this a dagger which I see before me, the handle toward my hand? . . . or art thou but a dagger of the mind . . .?

Faintly, there is the sound of a bell. Macbeth draws in his breath sharply.

MACBETH   I go, and it is done: the bell invites me. Hear it not, Duncan, for it is a knell that summons thee to Heaven, or to Hell.

Silently, he leaves the hall and begins to mount a stairway . . .
In the hall below, a softly gliding shadow appears. It is Lady
Macbeth. An owl cries.

LADY MACBETH   Hark! Peace! It was the owl that shrieked. (*She looks up*
toward the stairway, where Macbeth has vanished.) He is
about it: the doors are open, and the surfeited grooms do mock
their charge with snores. I have drugged their possets . . . Had
he not resembled my father as he slept, I had done it.

There is a slight noise. Macbeth descends the stairs.

MACBETH   I have done the deed.

LADY MACBETH   My husband!

MACBETH   (*staring at his bloody hands*) This is a sorry sight.

LADY MACBETH   A foolish thought, to say a sorry sight. Why did you bring these
daggers from the place? They must lie there; go carry them,
and smear the sleepy grooms with blood.

MACBETH   I'll go no more. I am afraid to think what I have done; look
on't again I dare not.

LADY MACBETH   Give me the daggers! The sleeping and the dead are but as
pictures. 'Tis the eye of childhood that fears a painted devil. If
he do bleed, I'll gild the faces of the grooms withal, for it must
seem their guilt!

She snatches the daggers and hastens away. Macbeth continues
to stare at his hands. Suddenly there is a loud knocking on the
castle's outer door.

MACBETH   Whence is that knocking? How is't with me, when every noise
appals me? Will all great Neptune's ocean wash this blood
clean from my hand? No, this my hand will rather the
multitudinous seas incarnadine, making the green one red!

Lady Macbeth returns. She holds up her hands. They are red.

LADY MACBETH   My hands are of your colour, but I shame to wear a heart so
white.

Again, the knocking.

LADY MACBETH Retire we to our chamber. A little water clears us of this deed. Get on your nightgown . . . Be not lost so poorly in your thoughts!

MACBETH To know my deed, 'twere best not know myself.

For a third time, comes the knocking.

MACBETH Wake Duncan with thy knocking: I would thou couldst!

The great door of the castle is opened. Macduff, the mighty Thane of Fife, with Lennox, a nobleman, have come to awaken the king. Macbeth, scrambled into night-attire, greets him.

MACDUFF Is the King stirring, worthy Thane?

MACBETH Not yet.

MACDUFF He did bid me to call timely upon him.

MACBETH I'll bring you to him.

He indicates the king's chamber and stands aside.

LENNOX Goes the King hence today?

MACBETH He does: he did appoint so.

LENNOX   The night has been unruly. Where we lay, our chimneys were blown down, and, as they say, lamentings heard i'the air; strange screams of death . . .

Macduff rushes out of the king's chamber.

MACDUFF   Horror, horror, horror! Awake, awake! Ring the alarum bell! Murder and treason!

Uproar and terror in the castle! Banquo, the king's sons and Lady Macbeth appear, white-faced, amazed. Macbeth rushes into the king's chamber.

LADY MACBETH   What's the business?

MACDUFF   Our royal master's murdered!

LADY MACBETH   Woe, alas! What! In our house?

Macbeth reappears. Malcolm and Donalbain, still tousled with sleep, enter.

DONALBAIN   What's amiss?

MACBETH   You are, and do not know it! The spring, the head, the fountain of your blood is stopped—

MACDUFF   Your royal father's murdered!

MALCOLM   O, by whom?

LENNOX   Those of his chamber, as it seemed, had done't. Their hands and faces were all badg'd with blood, so were their daggers—

MACBETH   O! yet do I repent me of my fury that I did kill them!

MACDUFF   Wherefore did you so?

All stare at Macbeth. Malcolm and Donalbain draw apart. They whisper fearfully.

MALCOLM   What will you do? I'll to England.

DONALBAIN   To Ireland, I. Our separated fortunes shall keep us both the safer; where we are, there's daggers in men's smiles; the near in blood, the nearer bloody.

Without a word, they vanish away like thieves in the night, leaving behind Macbeth, and the crown.

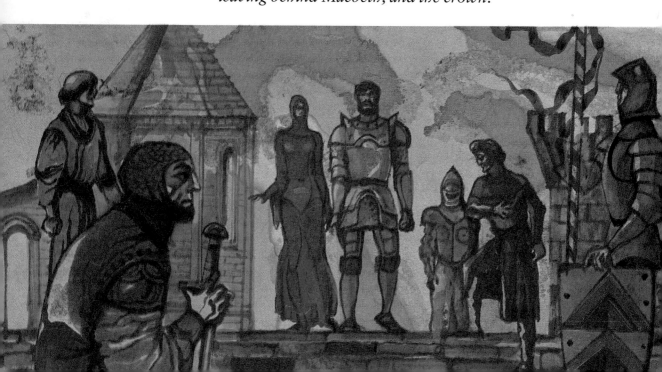

The crown of Scotland. In the great abbey church at Scone, the golden round, held in the trembling hands of a bishop, descends upon the head of Macbeth. Beside him kneels his queen. She is well satisfied. The second prophecy has been fulfilled. Yet her husband's face, far from triumphant, is bleak and haunted. He peers uneasily at the faces of the attending nobles. One, in particular, catches his eye. It is Banquo.

BANQUO   (*to himself*) Thou hast it now: King, Cawdor, Glamis, all, as the weird women promised, and I fear thou played'st most foully for it; yet it was said it should not stand in thy posterity, but that myself should be the root and father of many kings . . .

A room in the royal palace. There is to be a great feast to celebrate the crowning of Macbeth. All the great ones of Scotland have been bidden to attend. Among them is Banquo, and Fleance, his son. Macbeth smiles fondly at them.

MACBETH   Tonight we hold a solemn supper, sir, and I'll request your presence.

BANQUO   Let your highness command upon me.

MACBETH   Ride you this afternoon?

BANQUO   Ay, my good lord.

MACBETH   Is't far you ride?

BANQUO   As far, my lord, as will fill up the time 'twixt this and supper.

MACBETH   Goes Fleance with you?

BANQUO   Ay, my good lord.

MACBETH   Fail not our feast.

BANQUO   My lord, I will not.

Banquo and his son depart. Macbeth is alone. He goes to a window and stares out over the palace gardens.

MACBETH   To be thus is nothing, but to be safely thus. Our fears in Banquo stick deep . . .

He raises his hand. Below, two grim figures emerge from the concealment of bushes. They look up. Macbeth nods. They salute, and vanish. The door opens. Lady Macbeth enters and goes over to Macbeth.

LADY MACBETH   How now, my lord, why do you keep alone? Things without all remedy should be without regard; what's done is done.

MACBETH   We have scorched the snake, not killed it; she'll close and be herself . . . Better be with the dead, whom we, to gain our peace, have sent to peace. Duncan is in his grave; after life's fitful fever he sleeps well . . .

LADY MACBETH   You must leave this!

MACBETH   O! full of scorpions is my mind, dear wife! Thou knowest that Banquo and his Fleance lives.

LADY MACBETH   What's to be done?

MACBETH   Be innocent of the knowledge, dearest chuck, till thou applaud the deed. Come, seeling night, scarf up the tender eye of pitiful day, and with thy bloody and invisible hand cancel and tear to pieces that great bond which keeps me pale! Light thickens, and the crow makes wing to the rooky wood; good things of day begin to droop and drowse, whiles night's black agents to their prey do rouse. Thou marvel'st at my words, but hold thee still: things bad begun make strong themselves by ill.

The banqueting chamber. The flower of Scotland's nobility buzz and jostle in blossoming profusion. Sliding among them, serpent-like, Lady Macbeth darts her head from side to side, tasting the sweet air of royalty.

LADY MACBETH	You know your own degrees, sit down . . .
LORDS	Thanks to your Majesty!

They seat themselves at the great table. Music begins to play: the wild wailing of bagpipes and the rattle of a drum. A shadow lurks by the door: a muffled figure, beckoning. Macbeth observes it, and quietly approaches. The figure draws aside the covering of its face.

MACBETH	There's blood upon thy face.
MURDERER	'Tis Banquo's then.
MACBETH	Is he dispatched?
MURDERER	My lord, his throat is cut.
MACBETH	Thou art the best o' the cut-throats, yet he's good that did the like for Fleance!
MURDERER	Most royal sir, Fleance is scaped.
MACBETH	Then comes my fit again! I had else been perfect, but now I am cabined, cribbed, confined. But Banquo's safe?

MURDERER   Ay, my good lord; safe in a ditch he bides, with twenty trenched gashes on his head.

MACBETH   Thanks for that. Get thee gone.

The murderer, with a soldierly salute, vanishes away. Macbeth returns to his guests. He stares, puzzled, at the table.

LENNOX   May't please your highness, sit.

MACBETH   The table's full.

LENNOX   Here is a place reserved, sir.

MACBETH   Where?

LENNOX   Here, my good lord.

He gestures. Macbeth stares. In the offered place sits the ghost of Banquo!

MACBETH   Which of you have done this?

LORDS   What, my good lord?

The apparition raises its hand and points at Macbeth. Macbeth staggers in horror.

MACBETH   Thou canst not say I did it! Never shake thy gory locks at me!

Bewilderment at the table.

ROSSE Gentlemen, rise, his highness is not well!

LADY MACBETH Sit, worthy friends, my lord is often thus! Pray you keep seat! (*She goes to her husband's side, grasps him by the arm, and whispers fiercely*) Are you a man? This is the very painting of your fear! Why do you make such faces? When all's done, you look but on a stool!

MACBETH (*pointing at the apparition*) Prithee, see there! The time has been, that when the brains were out, the man would die, and there an end; but now they rise again, with twenty mortal murders on their crowns, and push us from our stools.

The ghost vanishes. Macbeth makes an effort to recover himself. He takes up a glass of wine, and offers a toast.

MACBETH Come, love and health to all! And to our dear friend Banquo, whom we miss! Would he were here!

He makes as if to drink. The music plays loudly; in particular, the drum. He glances at the drummer. It is Banquo! He hurls his glass at the ghost.

MACBETH   Avaunt, and quit my sight! Thy bones are marrowless, thy blood is cold; thou hast no speculation in those eyes which thou dost glare with! Hence, horrible shadow! Unreal mockery, hence!

A clatter of falling stools as everyone rises in alarm and amazement. A hubbub of voices, wondering what's amiss.

LADY MACBETH   I pray you, speak not! He grows worse and worse, question enrages him – at once, good night! Stand not upon the order of your going, but go at once!

Confusedly, the guests depart. Presently Macbeth and his wife are alone, amid the ruins of the feast.

MACBETH   It will have blood, they say: blood will have blood. What is the night?

LADY MACBETH   Almost at odds with morning, which is which.

MACBETH   How say'st thou, that Macduff denies his person at our great bidding?

LADY MACBETH   Did you send to him, sir?

MACBETH   I heard it by the way; but I will send. There's not a one of them
              but in his house I keep a servant fee'd. I will tomorrow to the
              weird sisters. More shall they speak; for I am bent to know by
              the worst means, the worst. I am in blood stepped in so far, that
              should I wade no more, returning were as tedious as going o'er.

LADY MACBETH You lack the season of all natures, sleep.

MACBETH   Come, we'll to sleep. We are yet but young in deed.

              Within a mean and smoky house, the three witches move
              slowly about a black cauldron that hisses and spits above a fire.
              As they revolve, they cast their strange offerings into the
              boiling pot.

1ST WITCH   Round about the cauldron go, in the poisoned entrails throw;
              toad that under cold stone days and nights has thirty-one.

ALL   Double, double, toil and trouble; fire burn and cauldron
              bubble.

2ND WITCH   Fillet of a fenny snake, in the cauldron boil and bake. Eye of
              newt and toe of frog, wool of bat and tongue of dog . . .

ALL   Double, double, toil and trouble; fire burn and cauldron
              bubble.

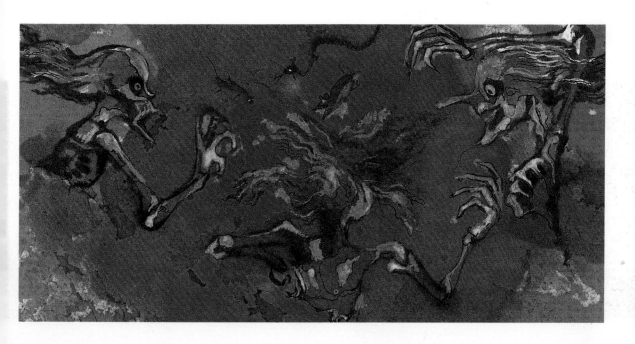

3RD WITCH   Finger of birth-strangled babe ditch-delivered by a drab, make the gruel thick and slab . . .

ALL   Double, double, toil and trouble; fire burn and cauldron bubble . . .

Comes a knocking on the door.

2ND WITCH   By the pricking of my thumbs, something wicked this way comes! Open, locks, whoever knocks!

The door opens. Macbeth enters. Vanished is the once noble warrior. His face is savage and depraved.

MACBETH   How now, you secret, black, and midnight hags? What is't you do?

ALL   A deed without a name.

MACBETH   Answer me to what I ask you.

1ST WITCH   Speak.

2ND WITCH   Demand.

3RD WITCH   We'll answer.

1ST WITCH   Say if th'hadst rather hear it from our mouths, or from our masters?

MACBETH   Call 'em; let me see 'em.

They nod. Then, from a homely jug, one of them pours blood into the cauldron. It spits in a fury. Dense vapours arise and out of the swirling air, a strange sight appears, to the accompaniment of thunder. It is a helmeted head.

1ST APPARITION   Macbeth, Macbeth, Macbeth, beware Macduff, beware the Thane of Fife.

The apparition vanishes. Macbeth nods grimly.

MACBETH   Thou hast harped my fear aright. But—

Thunder again. A second apparition. It is a bloody child.

2ND APPARITION   Macbeth, Macbeth, Macbeth, be bloody, bold and resolute. None of woman born shall harm Macbeth.

MACBETH   Then live Macduff – what need I fear of thee? But yet I'll make assurance double sure . . . thou shalt not live!

The second apparition dissolves away, and gives way, with a further, solemn roll of thunder, to a third apparition. It is a crowned child with a branch in its hand.

3RD APPARITION   Macbeth shall never vanquished be until great Birnam Wood to high Dunsinane Hill shall come against him. (*It vanishes.*)

MACBETH   That will never be. Who can impress the forest, bid the tree unfix his earth-bound root? Yet my heart throbs to know one thing: shall Banquo's issue ever reign in this kingdom?

ALL   Seek to know no more.

MACBETH   I will be satisfied!

Strange music. The fire dies, the cauldron sinks into the earth.

ALL   Show his eyes, and grieve his heart; come like shadows, so depart.

Out of the thick air stalks a procession of crowned kings. There are eight of them. Last of all comes murdered, bloody Banquo. Banquo points to the kings, then to himself, and smiles. The vision and the witches disappear. Macbeth is alone.

MACBETH   Where are they? Gone? Let this pernicious hour stand aye accursed in the calendar! (*There's a knocking on the door*) Come in, without there!

Lennox enters.

MACBETH   Saw you the weird sisters?

LENNOX   No, my lord.

MACBETH   Came they not by you?

LENNOX   No indeed, my lord.

MACBETH   Infected be the air whereon they ride, and damned all those that trust them! I did hear the galloping of horse. Who was't came by?

LENNOX   'Tis two or three, my lord, that bring you word Macduff is fled to England.

MACBETH   Time, thou anticipat'st my exploits! From this moment the very firstlings of my heart shall be the firstlings of my hand! The castle of Macduff I will surprise, seize upon Fife, give to the edge of the sword his wife, his babes, and all unfortunate souls that trace him in his line. No boasting like a fool; this deed I'll do before this purpose cool.

A room in the palace. Macbeth gazes out of his murderer's window, across a wide landscape, towards a distant castle on an eminence. He raises his hand. Tiny black figures, like malignant beetles, scurry across the green land and mount the hillside towards the castle. They reach it and swarm up its walls, finding little entrances and penetrating them. On the battlements they reappear, hurling white-gowned figures to their deaths. Tiny screams reach the watcher at the window, who nods . . .

A sunlit field in peaceful England. Malcolm and Macduff stand together.

MACDUFF   Not in the legions of horrid Hell can come a devil more damned in evils to top Macbeth.

MALCOLM   Our poor country sinks beneath the yoke. Here from gracious England have I offer of goodly thousands . . .

As they talk, a horseman approaches, weary and travel-stained. It is Rosse.

MALCOLM   My ever gentle cousin, welcome hither. Stands Scotland where it did?

ROSSE   Alas, poor country! The dead man's knell is there scarce asked for who, and good men's lives expire before the flowers in their caps.

MALCOLM	What's the newest grief?
MACDUFF	How does my wife?
ROSSE	Why, well.
MACDUFF	And all my children?
ROSSE	They were well at peace when I did leave 'em.
MACDUFF	Be not a niggard of your speech. Keep it not from me; quickly, let me have it.
ROSSE	Your castle is surprised; your wife and babes savagely slaughtered –
MALCOLM	Merciful Heaven!
MACDUFF	My children too?
ROSSE	Wife, children, servants, all that could be found.
MACDUFF	My wife killed too?
ROSSE	I have said.

MACDUFF   He has no children! Did you say all? – O Hell-kite! – All?
           What, all my pretty chickens and their dam at one fell swoop?

MALCOLM   Let grief convert to anger –

MACDUFF   Front to front bring you this fiend of Scotland and myself;
           within my sword's length set him!

MALCOLM   Our power is ready. Macbeth is ripe for shaking . . .

*The high dark castle of Dunsinane. It is night. In a quiet
ante-chamber, a doctor and a waiting-gentlewoman stand and
murmur together.*

DOCTOR   I have two nights watched with you, but can perceive no truth
           in your report. When was it –

*Even as he speaks, a flickering light approaches. It is a taper,
carried by Lady Macbeth. She is in her nightgown. As she
walks, she rubs her hands together, causing the taper to tilt and
cast wild shadows.*

WOMAN   Lo you, here she comes! This is her very guise, and upon my
           life, fast asleep.

DOCTOR   You see her eyes are open.

WOMAN   Ay, but their sense are shut.

DOCTOR   What is it she does now?

WOMAN   It is an accustomed action with her, to seem thus washing her
            hands: I have known her continue in this for a quarter of an
            hour.

LADY MACBETH   Look, here's a spot.

DOCTOR   Hark, she speaks.

LADY MACBETH   Out, damned spot! out, I say! — One; two: why, 'tis time to
                do't. — Fie, my lord, fie! a soldier, and afeard? — What need we
                fear who knows it, when none can call our power to accompt?
                — Yet who would have thought the old man to have had so
                much blood in him?

DOCTOR   Do you mark that?

LADY MACBETH   The Thane of Fife had a wife: where is she now? – What, will these hands ne'er be clean?

DOCTOR   Go to, go to, you have known what you should not!

WOMAN   She has spoke what she should not: I am sure of that; Heaven knows what she has known!

LADY MACBETH   Here's the smell of the blood still. All the perfumes of Arabia will not sweeten this little hand. O, O, O!

DOCTOR   What a sigh is there! The heart is sorely charged.

WOMAN   I would not have such a heart in my bosom for the dignity of the whole body.

DOCTOR   This disease is beyond my practice –

LADY MACBETH   Wash your hands, put on your nightgown; look not so pale. I tell you yet again, Banquo's buried: he cannot come out on's grave.

DOCTOR   Even so?

LADY MACBETH   To bed, to bed: there's knocking at the gate. Come, come, come, come, give me your hand. What's done cannot be undone. To bed, to bed, to bed . . .

                  She drifts away.

DOCTOR   More needs she the divine than the physician. God, God forgive us all!

                  Open country, near Dunsinane. Two Scottish nobles on horseback meet and exchange news.

1ST NOBLE   The English power is near, led on by Malcolm and the good Macduff.

2ND NOBLE   Near Birnam Wood we shall meet them.

1ST NOBLE   What does the tyrant?

2ND NOBLE   Great Dunsinane he strongly fortifies. Some say he's mad . . .

1ST NOBLE | Now does he feel his secret murders sticking on his hands. Those he commands move only in command, nothing in love. Now does he feel his title hang loose about him, like a giant's robe upon a dwarfish thief.

Dunsinane castle. In a fierce and warlike chamber, hung with swords and spears and shields, Macbeth, watched by the doctor and attendants, paces to and fro in furious agitation. A servant enters, trembling.

MACBETH | The devil damn thee black, thou cream-faced loon! Where got'st thou that goose-look?

SERVANT | There is ten thousand —

MACBETH | — Geese, villain?

SERVANT | Soldiers, sir. The English force —

MACBETH | — Take thy face hence! (*The servant, trembling, departs.*)

MACBETH | I am sick at heart. I have lived long enough: my way of life is fallen into the sere, the yellow leaf, and that which should accompany old age, as honour, love, obedience, troops of friends, I must not look to have; but in their stead, curses, not loud but deep, mouth-honour . . . (*He turns to the doctor.*) How does your patient, doctor?

DOCTOR   Not so sick, my lord, as she is troubled with thick-coming fancies, that keep her from her rest.

MACBETH   Cure her of that: canst thou not minister to a mind diseased, pluck from the memory a rooted sorrow, raze out the written troubles of the brain, and with some sweet oblivious antidote cleanse the stuffed bosom of that perilous stuff which weighs upon the heart?

DOCTOR   Therein the patient must minister to himself.

MACBETH   Throw physic to the dogs; I'll none of it! (*He turns to his attendants.*) Come, put mine armour on! I'll fight till from my bones my flesh be hacked! Till Birnam Wood remove to Dunsinane, I cannot taint with fear!

The English force, led by Malcolm and Macduff, and a company of Scottish nobles. Before them stands a forest . . .

NOBLE   What wood is this before us?

2ND NOBLE The Wood of Birnam.

MALCOLM   Let every soldier hew him down a bough, and bear it before him.

The order is passed. The soldiers advance and, with swords and axes, cripple the trees, leaving white wounds, like dead men's faces. Presently, another forest, it seems, begins to move across the land . . .

The courtyard of Dunsinane castle. A warlike scene. Macbeth in armour, with soldiers about him. Banners fly, drums roll.

MACBETH   Hang out our banners on the outward walls!

There is a sudden cry of women from high up in the castle.

MACBETH   What is that noise?

COURTIER   It is the cry of women, my good lord. (*He goes to discover the cause.*)

MACBETH   I have almost forgot the taste of fears: the time has been, my senses would have cooled to hear a night-shriek, and my fell of hair would at a dismal treatise rise and stir as life were in it. I have supped full with horrors . . .

The courtier returns. His face is grave.

MACBETH   Wherefore was that cry?

COURTIER   The Queen, my lord, is dead.

MACBETH   She should have died hereafter; there would have been a time for such a word. Tomorrow, and tomorrow, and tomorrow creeps in this petty pace from day to day, to the last syllable of recorded time: and all our yesterdays have lighted fools the way to dusty death. Out, out brief candle! Life's but a walking shadow, a poor player that struts and frets his hour upon this stage, and then is heard no more. It is a tale told by an idiot, full of sound and fury, signifying nothing.

A soldier approaches, staring-eyed.

MACBETH   Thou com'st to use thy tongue; thy story quickly!

SOLDIER   As I did stand my watch upon the hill, I looked toward Birnam, and anon methought the wood began to move!

MACBETH	Liar and slave!
SOLDIER	Within this three mile you may see it coming; I say, a moving grove!
MACBETH	If thou speak'st false . . . (*The man shakes his head violently. Macbeth dismisses him.*) I begin to doubt the equivocation of the fiend that lies like truth. 'Fear not till Birnam Wood do come to Dunsinane,' and now a wood comes towards Dunsinane. Arm, arm, and out! If this which he avouches does appear, there is no flying hence or tarrying here. I gin to be a-weary of the sun, and wish the estate of the world were now undone. Ring the alarum bell! Blow, wind! come wrack, at least we'll die with harness on our back!

He draws his sword and, with a shout of defiance, rushes from the castle, leading his soldiers down to the forest of trees that moves inexorably towards him.

The hillside. With furious shouts, the army of Macbeth rushes down towards the ever-oncoming wood. Suddenly, the leafy boughs are flung aside, and the forces of Malcolm and Macduff are revealed. In moments, the battle is engaged. The air is full of shrieks and shouts and bitter steel, and whirling dust. Macbeth in the midst, plying his trade of war with a giant's arm and strength.

MACBETH   They have tied me to the stake; I cannot fly, but bear-like I must fight the course.

A warrior confronts him. They fight. The warrior is slain.

MACBETH   What's he that was not born of woman? Such a one am I to fear, or none!

On another part of the hill, Macduff seeks Macbeth.

MACDUFF   That way the noise is. Tyrant, show thy face. If thou be'st slain, and with no stroke of mine, my wife and children's ghosts will haunt me still. I cannot strike at wretched kerns, whose arms are hired to bear their staves. Either thou, Macbeth, or else my sword with an unbattered edge I sheathe again undeeded. There thou shouldst be: by this great clatter one of greatest note seems bruited. Let me find him, fortune! and more I beg not.

He sees Macbeth.

MACDUFF   Turn, hell-hound, turn!

MACBETH   (*turning*) Of all men else I have avoided thee. But get thee back! My soul is too much charged with blood of thine already!

MACDUFF   I have no words; my voice is in my sword, thou bloodier villain than terms can give thee out.

They fight.

MACBETH   Thou losest labour. I bear a charmed life, which must not yield to one of woman born!

MACDUFF   Despair thy charm, and let the Angel whom thou still hast served, tell thee, Macduff was from his mother's womb untimely ripped!

MACBETH   Accursed be that tongue that tells me so, for it hath cowed my better part of man! And be these juggling fiends no more believed, that palter with us in a double sense, that keep the word of promise to our ear, and break it to our hope. I'll not fight with thee.

MACDUFF   Then yield thee, coward; and live to be the show and gaze o'the time. We'll have thee, as our rarer monsters are, painted upon a pole, and underwrit, 'Here may you see the tyrant.'

MACBETH   I will not yield. Though Birnam Wood be come to Dunsinane, and thou opposed, being of no woman born, yet will I try the last! Before my body I throw my warlike shield: lay on, Macduff, and damned be him that first cries, 'Hold, enough!'

They fight, and vanish into the clouds of dust, fighting. Suddenly there is a cry of dismay. The air thins and the head of Macbeth rises up, fierce and unrepentant. But the head is all. It has been severed at the neck, and is fixed upon the sword of Macduff.

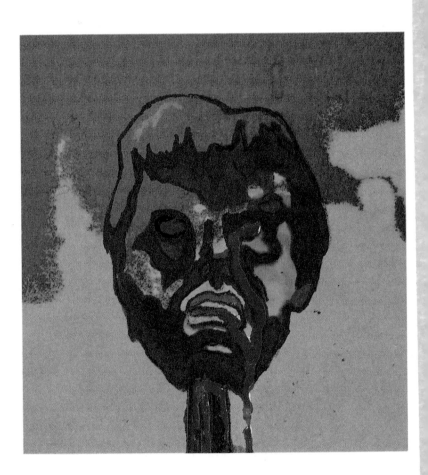

There is a mighty shout of joy. Macbeth is dead: the battle has been lost and won.

The curtain falls . . .